M000074526

CHOCOLATE HEAVEN

Steven Wheeler

RIZZOLI
NEW YORK

First published in the United States of America in 1995 by
RIZZOLI INTERNATIONAL PUBLICATIONS, INC.
300 Park Avenue South, New York, NY 10010

First published in Germany in 1995 by
DuMont Buchverlag

ISBN   0-8478-1896-9
LC 95-67263

Photos: Kulbir Thandi

Printed in Italy

CONTENTS

THE HISTORY OF CHOCOLATE

Chocolate was first known of as 'liquid gold' and was treasured as a commodity.

The cocoa tree (*Theobroma cacao*) has grown in the Amazon Basin in South America for more than four thousand years. The Maya, an ancient tribal race, harvested the bean and paid it in 'tribute' to the conquering Aztecs

from the south. The Aztecs believed that chocolate had a divine quality. The Aztec god, Quetzalcoatl, is said to have taught them how to make chocolate from the cocoa trees and chocolate played an essential part in their religious ceremonies.

Christopher Columbus was the first European to taste chocolate, but he was unimpressed with the dark, bitter drink. It was Hernan Cortes, 17 years later, who is credited with bringing the cocoa bean back to the Old World. When Cortes first landed in Mexico in 1519, the Aztec emperor, Montezuma II, offered him a dark drink called *xocolatl*. Later Cortes described a banquet given by the emperor, at which about 50 large bowls of cacao were drunk.

Montezuma was clearly the first in a long line of chocolate enthusiasts.

The Spaniards in Mexico quickly acquired a taste for the drink, adding sugar, cinnamon and vanilla to it. When first introduced to Spain, it was reserved for the Court alone, its recipe a secret known only to the monks who were entrusted with its preparation.

Gradually, however, its popularity spread throughout Europe and chocolate houses became the rage. The first one appeared in London in 1657, and was quickly followed by similar establishments throughout the fashionable cities of Europe. Chocolate houses attracted all social classes and some were even infamous gambling dens.

Bars of chocolate as we know them were not invented until the industrialization of Europe, when machines for grinding the beans became available and the chocolate-making process moved into factories. In 1828 the Dutch firm of Van Houten revolutionized the chocolate industry by developing a way to extract the cocoa butter from the beans, enabling a less rich and more palatable drink to be produced. The inventor of 'eating chocolate' is unknown, but a British manufacturer, J. S. Fry, sold a *chocolat délicieux à manger* in 1847 and two years later the Cadbury brothers were selling a similar product. Chocolate-lovers had to wait another 25 years, however, before the Swiss manufacturers Daniel Peter and Henri Nestlé first introduced milk chocolate to the market.

MALTED CHOCOLATE MOUSSE

*This wonderful mousse includes a little malt extract
to give it a special richness and flavour. Malt extract
is available in most health food stores.*

SERVES 4

*200 g / 7 oz good quality plain (semi-
   sweet) chocolate, broken into
   pieces
3 eggs, separated
30 ml / 1 floz / 2 tbsp malt extract
30 ml / 2 tbsp caster (superfine) sugar
300 ml / ½ pint / 1¼ cups double
   (heavy) cream, loosely whipped*

For the decoration

*150 ml / ¼ pint / ⅔ cup whipping
   cream, loosely whipped
75 g / 3 oz plain (semi-sweet)
   chocolate, flaked (see page 76)
icing (confectioner's) sugar*

Melt the chocolate in a bowl set over a saucepan of gently simmering water. Remove the melted chocolate from the heat. Add the egg yolks and stir in the malt extract.

Place the egg whites in a large mixing bowl. Whisk the egg whites with the sugar until soft peaks form. Pour the melted chocolate mixture into the whisked egg whites and fold in gently with a metal spoon. Add the whipped cream and fold in evenly.

Turn the mixture into serving glasses and decorate with swirls of whipped cream, flaked chocolate and a dusting of sifted icing sugar. Chill for 40 minutes, or until firm.

*P*UITS D'AMOUR AU CHOCOLAT

*Puits d'amour is for lovers - translated it means 'well of love.'
A crisp pastry case holds a heavenly chocolate mixture
with a topping of macaroons.*

SERVES 2

*175 g / 6 oz ready-prepared puff
    pastry, thawed if frozen*
soft butter for greasing

For the chocolate filling
2 eggs, separated
150 ml / ¼ pint / ⅔ cup milk
45 ml / 3 tbsp plain (all-purpose) flour
*75 g / 3 oz plain (semi-sweet)
    chocolate, chopped or grated*
*30 ml / 2 tbsp caster (superfine)
    sugar*

For the decoration
25 g / 1 oz crushed macaroons

Grease a 13cm / 5in fluted flan tin (quiche pan) with butter. Roll out the pastry on a floured surface and use to line the tin (pan). Trim the top edge and prick the base well with a fork. Line with grease proof (wax) paper or foil and fill with baking beans. Chill for 45 minutes. Preheat the oven to 180°C / 375°F / Gas 5. Bake the pastry case (shell) for 20-25 minutes until crisp and dry. Leave to cool.

To make the filling, place the egg yolks in a medium-sized bowl and the whites in a large bowl. Add 45 ml / 3 tbsp of the milk to the egg yolks, add the flour and stir until smooth. Bring the remainder of the milk to the boil with the chocolate, pour into the egg yolk mixture and blend well. Return to the pan and cook gently, stirring until thickened. Cover and set aside.

Whisk the egg whites, add the sugar and whisk thoroughly until firm. Stir a spoonful of the hot mixture into the egg whites, then fold in the remainder. Turn into the baked pastry case and cool. Top with the macaroons.

CHOCOLATE CHERRY ROULADE

Happiness is a chocolate roulade studded with black cherries and wound with a spiral of cream.

SERVES 4

For the sponge

3 eggs, at room temperature

75 g / 3 oz / ⅓ cup caster (superfine)
  sugar

45 ml / 3 tbsp ground almonds, sifted

60 ml / 4 tbsp cocoa

15 ml / 1 tbsp cornflour (cornstarch)

For the filling

650 g / 22 oz bottled black cherries,
  pitted

45 ml / 3 tbsp Maraschino or Kirsch

300 ml / ½ pint / 1¼ cups double
  (heavy) cream

30 ml / 2 tbsp vanilla sugar

icing (confectioner's) sugar

Preheat the oven to 200°C / 400°F / Gas 6. Line the base of a 33 x 25cm / 13 x 10in Swiss roll (jelly roll) tray with greaseproof (wax) paper. Whisk the eggs and sugar in a bowl until the mixture leaves a thick trail across the surface. Add the sifted ground almonds, cocoa and cornflour, then fold in gently with a metal spoon. Turn the mixture into the prepared tray, spread to the corners and bake for 10-12 minutes until springy to the touch. Leave to cool.

Drain the cherries and soak in the alcohol. Sweeten the cream with the vanilla sugar, then whip loosely. Place a piece of greaseproof (wax) paper on a clean work surface. Turn the sponge onto it and peel off the lining paper.

Spread the cream over the sponge and dot with cherries. To roll, lift the short end of the paper to encourage the sponge to roll. Turn onto a plate and serve dusted with icing (confectioner's) sugar.

THE CHOCOLATE TREE

*The source of chocolate is
the dark brown bean of the cocoa plant.*

The tree that produces the cocoa bean, *Theobroma cacao* ('the food of the gods'), grows in many tropical regions but principally in West Africa. Each large pod, which is the fruit of the tree, contains up to 40 beans. The beans are fermented and dried before being shipped to chocolate manufacturers throughout the world.

Once arrived, the beans are roasted before being broken down and sieved into small pieces, a process known as kibbling and winnowing. The resulting pieces of  beans are known as 'nibs'. At this point, the nibs are usually alkalized (Dutch processed) to further develop their flavour and

colour. They are then ground to produce a thick liquid, known as 'mass', which contains 55-58% cocoa butter. At this stage cocoa and chocolate go their separate ways.

COCOA PRODUCTION

Cocoa powder is made by extracting a portion of the cocoa butter from the 'mass'. The solid block of cocoa remaining after extraction is pulverized to produce cocoa powder.

Cocoa has a good bitter flavour but needs to be sweetened before it becomes palatable in drinks. Since cocoa contains starch, it should be mixed to a paste with a little cold water or milk (or as instructed in a recipe) before it is added to a hot liquid.

Boiling cocoa for a few minutes and then whisking it vigorously to a velvety froth improves its flavour and digestibility.

In the USA, cocoa is traditionally drunk with a topping of whipped cream or melting marshmallow.

Mocha, a mixture of cocoa and coffee, is a favourite Russian winter drink.

CHOCOLATE PRODUCTION

The precise chocolate-making process varies not only from country to country, but also from one chocolatier to another. Essentially, though, the cocoa 'mass' is refined with extra cocoa butter and sugar. Grinding between rollers then reduces the particle size, followed by conching, a wavelike motion which further removes unwanted volatile oils, develops flavour and coats the sugar and cocoa particles with cocoa butter. The chocolate is then tempered by alternate heating and cooling, and finally flavoured and shaped as required.

Europeans originally enjoyed chocolate purely as a beverage and by 1700 it was a fashionable breakfast drink, sweetened with sugar and flavoured with cinnamon and vanilla. Several early French and English recipes have survived which explain how to prepare drinking chocolate. Real enthusiasts even had a special pot for chocolate, which was milled with a 'molinquet', or wooden stick, to bring up the froth.

*C*HOCOLATE MONT BLANC

Reflected in the still waters of Lake Geneva is a sugar-white mountain skyline peaked with snow - Mont Blanc is its summit. Here, this beautiful 'mountain' is fashioned with chestnut purée, cream, Kirsch and meringue topped with dark chocolate shavings.

SERVES 4

For the topping

75 ml / 3 floz / ¹/₃ cup water

30 ml / 2tbsp caster (superfine) sugar

75 g / 3 oz plain (semi-sweet)
* chocolate, chopped*

75 g / 3 oz sweetened chestnut purée

15 ml / 1 tbsp Kirsch

300 ml / ¹/₂ pint / 1¹/₄ cups double
* (heavy) cream, loosely whipped*

For the base

4 sponge (lady) fingers

45 ml / 3 tbsp Kirsch

4 ready-prepared meringue bases

For the decoration

chocolate shavings (see page 76)

To make the topping, bring the water and sugar to the boil in a small saucepan, stirring to dissolve the sugar. Remove from the heat, add the chocolate and stir until melted. Set aside to cool.

In a small bowl, combine the chestnut purée with the Kirsch, then fold in half of the loosely whipped cream. Fold the remainder of the cream into the cool chocolate mixture.

Place a perforated worm cast icing tube into a piping (icing) bag. Spoon the chestnut mixture into one side of the bag and the chocolate mixture into the other.

Moisten the sponge (lady) fingers with the Kirsch and position over the 4 meringue bases. Pipe the toppings into a 'mountain' over the sponge and decorate with chocolate shavings.

CHOCOLATE HONEY CAKES

Honey and spice add flavour to these pretty dark-chocolate-coated hearts - sure to rekindle lost passions!

MAKES 4

150 g / 5 oz / 1 ¼ cups strong white bread flour

75 g / 3 oz / ⅔ cup rye flour

1½ tsp bicarbonate of soda (baking soda)

½ tsp salt

½ tsp aniseed

½ tsp ground cinnamon

½ tsp ground coriander

1 tsp mustard powder

¼ tsp ground allspice

¼ tsp ground mace

225 g / 8 oz / ⅔ cup clear honey

50 g / 2 oz white marzipan, chopped

50 ml / 2 floz / ¼ cup water

3 egg yolks

300 g / 11 oz plain (semi-sweet) chocolate, broken into pieces

Preheat the oven to 160°c / 325°F / Gas 3. Line a 23cm / 9 in square cake tin (pan) with greaseproof (wax) paper and set aside. Sift the two flours, bicarbonate of soda (baking soda) and salt into a bowl.

Crush the aniseed using a pestle and mortar, add the other spices and mix with the flour. Warm the honey by standing the jar in a saucepan of gently simmering water for 3-4 minutes. Add the honey, marzipan, water and egg yolks to the flour mixture and beat to form a firm batter.

Turn the mixture into the prepared cake tin (pan) and bake for 40-50 minutes until it is springy to the touch. Turn out and cool on a wire rack.

When the cake is completely cool, trim level and cut out 4 heart shapes. Melt the chocolate in a bowl set over simmering water. Temper the chocolate following the method

described on page 77. Spread a sheet of greaseproof (wax) paper on a tray. Place one honey-cake heart at a time on a fork, then spoon the melted chocolate over it. Tap the fork on the side of the bowl to ensure an even covering on the cake. Leave on the covered tray until the chocolate has set. (In summer months leave in the refrigerator to set.)

℘ETITS PÔTS DE CHOCOLAT

These smooth custard creams are made decadently rich with generous
amounts of dark chocolate and cream.

MAKES 8

600 ml / 1 pint / 2 ½ cups very fresh
  single (light) cream
4 egg yolks
1 egg
50 g / 2 oz / ¼ cup caster (superfine)
  sugar
45 ml / 3 tbsp water
225 g / 8 oz plain (semi-sweet)
  chocolate, broken into pieces

Preheat the oven to 180°c /350°F/ Gas 4. Arrange 8 x 75 ml / 3 floz capacity custard pots or ramekin dishes in a roasting tin (pan) and set aside.

Bring the cream almost to the boil in a heavy saucepan that has been rinsed with cold water to prevent sticking. Combine 3 egg yolks, the whole egg and 25 g / 1 oz / 5 tsp of the sugar in a bowl.

Pour in the heated cream and stir evenly.

Place the water and the remaining sugar in a small saucepan and bring to the boil, stirring constantly to dissolve the sugar. Remove from the heat, add the chocolate and stir gently until completely melted. Mix in the remaining egg yolk.

Combine the melted chocolate mixture with the cream, strain into a jug and fill the custard pots to the brim. Half-fill the roasting tin (pan) with boiling water and bake the chocolate pots for 25-30 minutes until set. Cool, then chill before serving.

ℱALLEN ANGEL

*Dark chocolate blends well with the soft flesh of the fig
to give a deliciously smooth foretaste of heaven.*

SERVES 4-6

2 eggs, at room temperature

50 g / 2 oz / ¼ cup caster (superfine)
sugar

30 ml / 2 tbsp plain (all-purpose)
flour

30 ml / 2 tbsp cornflour (cornstarch)

60 ml / 4 tbsp seedless raspberry jam

For the filling

250 g / 9 oz plain (semi-sweet)
chocolate, broken into pieces

45 ml / 3 tbsp double (heavy) cream

60 ml / 4 tbsp Grand Marnier

25 g / 1 oz / 2 tbsp candied orange
peel, chopped

25 g / 1 oz / ¼ cup amaretti biscuits,
crushed

8 fresh figs

Preheat the oven to 220°C/425°F/
Gas 7. Grease and line the base of a 33 x 25 cm / 13 x 10 in Swiss roll (jelly roll) tray with greaseproof (wax) paper. Whisk the eggs and sugar together until the mixture leaves a thick trail on the surface. Sift the plain flour and cornflour onto the eggs and fold in gently with a metal spoon.

Transfer the mixture to the prepared tray and spread into the corners. Bake for 10-12 minutes until springy to the touch. Leave to cool.

To make the filling, melt the chocolate in a bowl set over a saucepan of simmering water. Add the cream and Grand Marnier, stir well and leave to cool completely.

Place an 18 cm / 7 in flan ring on a baking sheet lined with greaseproof (wax) paper, then line the ring. Remove the paper from the cooled sponge, then cut a 16 cm / 6¼ in circle of cake and place it inside the

ring. Cut the remaining sponge into 4 cm / 1½ in strips. Sandwich the strips with raspberry jam so that they are as tall as they are wide. Place the strips in the freezer to firm for 1 hour.

Cut the sponge strips into 5 mm / ¼ in slices. Line the sides of the ring with sponge slices, alternating the layers (upright, horizontal, upright).

When the chocolate mixture has firmed, stir in the crushed amaretti and orange peel, then spread into the lined flan ring. Chill to firm and decorate with sections of fresh fig.

TYPES OF CHOCOLATE

There is an immense variety of types of chocolate,
for every taste and culinary or decorative use.

Chocolate is classified according to whether sugar is added to the original cocoa mass, and in what quantity, and whether it contains milk. Any chocolate lover knows that brands differ enormously, and everyone will have their own favourite. Differences between brands are due to each company's unique formula for blending beans and mixing chocolate solids. Taste and texture are also affected by the length of roasting, grinding and conching (grinding between rollers to improve texture). The characteristic velvety-smooth texture of European chocolate, particularly Swiss, is the result of up to 96 hours of conching. In contrast, American chocolate may be conched for as little as 4-5 hours.

CHOCOLAT PAYRAUD

UNSWEETENED (PURE) CHOCOLATE

Pure chocolate contains cocoa mass with only a little cocoa butter added and gives excellent results in cooking. It is not easily available but can be specially ordered from suppliers.

COCOA

Cocoa is pure cocoa mass with about two-thirds of the cocoa butter removed. Most European cocoa is Dutch-processed, meaning that it has been treated with a mild alkali to mellow the flavour.

needs to be 'tempered' before it can be used, which involves a complicated heating / cooling / heating process, described on page 77.

PLAIN OR DARK (BITTER-SWEET / SEMI-SWEET) CHOCOLATE

Dark chocolate is pure cocoa mass with sugar and extra cocoa butter added. The higher the percentage of cocoa solids (cocoa mass and cocoa butter), the better the quality of chocolate. Swiss, French and Belgian chocolate typically have a high proportion of cocoa solids. British 'plain' chocolate is less rich with the minimum 34% cocoa solids.

COUVERTURE

This is a high-quality confectioner's product. The high percentage of cocoa butter in couverture gives it a low melting point, making it the ideal chocolate for coating and decorative work. However, it

MILK CHOCOLATE

Milk chocolate is produced in a similar way to plain chocolate but has less cocoa mass and instead contains either condensed or dried milk. It is much sweeter and milder in flavour than plain chocolate.

WHITE CHOCOLATE

Although white chocolate does not contain any cocoa mass, it does contain up to 30% cocoa butter plus milk, sugar and flavourings and can therefore still be classified as 'real chocolate'. It is generally very sweet. Inferior brands use vegetable oil instead of cocoa butter, so check the packaging carefully.

GÂTEAU OPÉRA

A night at the opera is matched only by this decadent display of dark chocolate, coffee cream and sponge richly decorated with gold leaf.

SERVES 4-6

2 eggs, at room temperature

50 g / 2 oz / ¼ cup caster (superfine)
 sugar

30 ml / 2 tbsp cornflour (cornstarch)

45 ml / 3 tbsp ground almonds

45 ml / 3 tbsp cocoa

For the chocolate filling

250 ml / 8 floz / 1 cup double
 (heavy) cream

115 g / 4 oz / ½ cup caster
 (superfine) sugar

275 g / 10 oz plain (semi-sweet)
 chocolate, broken into pieces

15 ml / 1 tbsp Cognac

For the coffee filling

250 ml / 8 floz / 1 cup double
 (heavy) cream

115 g / 4 oz / ½ cup caster
 (superfine) sugar

275 g / 10 oz white chocolate

15 ml / 1 tbsp strong black coffee

300 g / 11 oz plain (semi-sweet)
 chocolate

gold leaf (optional)

Preheat the oven to 220°C / 425°F /
Gas 7. Line the base of a 30 cm /
12 in square cake tin (pan) with
greaseproof (wax) paper. Whisk the
eggs and sugar together until thick.
Sift the cornflour, ground almonds
and cocoa onto the eggs and fold in.
Turn into the cake tin (pan), and
bake for 10-12 minutes or until
springy to the touch. Cool.

To make the chocolate filling, rinse
a saucepan with cold water, add the
cream and sugar and bring almost to
the boil. Remove from the heat, add
the chocolate and Cognac and stir
until melted. Leave to cool and firm.

To make the coffee filling, follow
the same procedure, substituting the

white chocolate and coffee for the plain chocolate and Cognac.

To assemble, cut the sponge into four thin layers. Layer the squares and fillings, finishing with a layer of chocolate filling. Chill for 30-40 minutes until firm.

Temper the plain chocolate as described on page 77. Trim the sides of the sponge with a serrated knife to neaten. Coat with the melted chocolate. Allow to set before piping the word 'Opera' in chocolate. Decorate with gold leaf (if desired).

BLACK FOREST GÂTEAU

This splendid gâteau is made with layers of chocolate sponge, cream, cherries and Kirsch garnished with fresh stemmed cherries.

SERVES 4

soft butter for greasing

2 eggs, at room temperature

50 g / 2 oz / ¼ cup caster (superfine)
  sugar

30 ml / 2 tbsp plain (all-purpose) flour

30 ml / 2 tbsp cocoa

30 ml / 2 tbsp ground almonds

½ tsp salt

200 g / 7 oz bottled black cherries,
  pitted

60 ml / 4 tbsp Kirsch

450 ml / ¾ pint / 1⅞ cups double
  (heavy) cream

30 ml / 2 tbsp vanilla sugar

225 g / 8 oz plain (semi-sweet)
  chocolate, flaked (see page 76)

4-6 fresh black cherries (with stalks)

icing (confectioner's) sugar

Preheat the oven to 190°c /
375°F / Gas 5. Grease a 15 cm /
6 in round, deep cake tin (pan). Line
the base with greaseproof (wax)
paper and dust the sides with flour.

Whisk the eggs and sugar until
thick. Add the flour, cocoa, almonds
and salt, then fold in. Turn into the
tin (pan) and bake for 25 minutes.
Cool on a rack.

Soak the bottled cherries in the
Kirsch. Loosely whip the cream with
the vanilla sugar. Slice the sponge
into three layers. Reserve a fourth of
the cream. Moisten the base layer of
sponge with Kirsch from the cherries.
Cover with cream and some cherries.
Sandwich with a second layer of
sponge, moisten with Kirsch and
cover with cream and cherries as
before. Assemble the final layer, then
cover the top and sides with cream
and flaked chocolate. Dust with icing
sugar.

Pipe on the reserved cream and top
with the fresh cherries.

SACHERTORTE

The sachertorte was first made by Franz Sacher in 1832 for the Viennese diplomat Metternich who had a passion for good chocolate.

SERVES 6-8

soft butter for greasing

175 g / 6 oz plain (semi-sweet) chocolate

75 g / 3 oz / ⅓ cup unsalted (sweet) butter, softened

75 g / 3 oz white marzipan, warmed

4 eggs, separated

30 ml / 2 tbsp Grand Marnier

50 g / 2 oz / ½ cup caster (superfine) sugar

2 oz / 50 g / ¼ cup plain (all-purpose) flour

¼ tsp salt

90 ml / 6 tbsp seedless raspberry jam

To finish

100 g / 4 oz white marzipan

45 ml / 3 tbsp water

60 ml / 4 tbsp caster (superfine) sugar

175 g / 6 oz plain (semi-sweet) chocolate

Preheat the oven to 180°C / 350°F / Gas 4. Grease a 23 cm / 9 in loose-bottomed cake tin (pan). Line the base with a circle of greaseproof (wax) paper and dust with flour.

Melt the chocolate over simmering water. Beat the butter and marzipan together, then add the egg yolks and Grand Marnier. Stiffly whisk the egg whites, gradually add the sugar and whisk until firm. Sift the flour and salt onto the egg whites and fold in.

Stir the melted chocolate into the butter, marzipan and egg yolk mixture, then fold into the beaten egg whites. Turn into the pan. Bake for 30 minutes, or until cake has shrunk from the side of the tin (pan). Cool on a wire rack, then remove the paper, split the sponge and sandwich with half of the raspberry jam. Place the cake upside down on the base of the cake tin (pan) and spread with the remaining jam.

To finish, roll the marzipan to a 23 cm / 9 in round and place over the jam. Place the cake on a wire rack set over a tray. To make the glaze, gently bring the water and sugar to a simmer in a small saucepan, then remove from the heat, add 150 g / 5 oz of the chocolate and stir to melt. Pour the glaze over the sponge and spread evenly. Allow to set. Finally, melt the remaining chocolate in a cup, thicken with a drop or two of water and pipe the word 'Sacher' across the top.

RICH CHOCOLATE CHEESECAKE

Extravagant, indulgent and so very delicious,
this cheesecake is for chocoholics everywhere.

SERVES 4-6

40 g / 1½ oz / 3 tbsp unsalted
(sweet) butter
75 g / 3 oz / ¾ cup digestive biscuit
(graham cracker) crumbs
75 ml / 3 floz / ⅓ cup double (heavy)
cream
225 g / 8 oz plain (semi-sweet)
chocolate, broken into pieces
30 ml / 2 tbsp dark rum
450 g / 1 lb medium-fat soft cheese
(cream cheese)
2 eggs
30 ml / 2 tbsp caster (superfine) sugar
30 ml / 2 tbsp clear honey
2 tsp plain (all-purpose) flour
45 ml / 3 tbsp cocoa
white and dark chocolate shavings
(see page 76)

Preheat the oven to 180°C / 350°F / Gas 4. Grease a 15 cm / 6 in springform tin (pan) and line the base with greaseproof (wax) paper. Melt the butter in a saucepan, then stir in the biscuit (cracker) crumbs. Spread onto the base of the cake tin (pan) and press firmly with the back of a spoon.

Rinse a small saucepan with cold water, add the cream and bring almost to the boil. Remove from the heat. Add the chocolate, stir until melted, then add the rum.

Beat the cheese, eggs, sugar and honey together. Add the flour and cocoa, then the melted chocolate. Combine well.

Turn the mixture into the prepared cake tin (pan), place on a baking sheet and bake for 50 minutes. Leave to cool completely before decorating with white and dark chocolate shavings.

$\mathcal{G}$ANACHE BAR

Here a sinfully rich mixture of dark chocolate and cream forms a tempting topping and is also captured between layers of light sponge.

SERVES 6-8

For the sponge
2 eggs, at room temperature
50 g / 2 oz / ¼ cup caster (superfine) sugar
30 ml / 2 tbsp cornflour (cornstarch)
45 ml / 3 tbsp ground almonds
45 ml / 3 tbsp cocoa

For the filling
300 ml / ½ pint/1¼ cups fresh double (heavy) cream
115 g / 4 oz / ½ cup caster (superfine) sugar
275 g / 10 oz plain (semi-sweet) chocolate, broken into pieces

To finish
30 ml / 2 tbsp cocoa
15 ml / 1 tbsp icing (confectioner's) sugar

Preheat the oven to 220°C/425°F/ Gas 7. Line the base of a 30 cm / 12 in square cake tin (pan) with greaseproof (wax) paper. Whisk the eggs and sugar together until the mixture leaves a thick trail on the surface. Sift the cornflour, ground almonds and cocoa onto the mixture and fold in gently with a metal spoon.

Turn into the lined cake tin (pan), spread into the corners and bake for 10-12 minutes until springy to the touch. Leave to cool.

To make the filling, rinse a saucepan with cold water, add the cream and sugar and bring almost to the boil. Remove from the heat, add the chocolate and stir until melted. Leave to cool and firm.

Turn the chocolate sponge upside down, remove the paper and cut the sponge into three equal strips. Sandwich the strips with a generous layer of

filling, and then also coat the top and sides with a layer of ganache filling.

Put the remaining filling in a piping (icing) bag fitted with a 1 cm / ½ in plain tube and pipe the filling in rows across the top. If the filling is too firm, warm it slightly and beat until it has a smooth consistency. Combine the cocoa and icing (confectioner's) sugar and use to dust over the surface.

$\mathscr{T}$IRAMISÙ CIOCCOLATO

This Italian dessert is shamelessly rich and delicious.
Black coffee and Marsala mingle with sponge fingers
beneath a layer of mascarpone cheese and chocolate.

SERVES 4

8 sponge (lady) fingers

150 ml / ¼ pint / ⅔ cup strong, black
   espresso coffee

75 ml / 3 floz / 4 tbsp Marsala

2 eggs

30 ml / 2 tbsp caster (superfine) sugar

225 g / 8 oz mascarpone cheese

For the decoration

50 g / 2 oz plain (semi-sweet)
   chocolate, flaked (see page 76)

cocoa, sifted

Break the sponge (lady) fingers into pieces and put into 4 serving glasses. Combine the coffee with the Marsala and pour over the sponge (lady) fingers.

Whisk the eggs and sugar together until thick and foamy. Stir a spoonful of the egg mixture into the mascarpone to soften, then fold in the remainder.

Spoon the cheese mixture over the moistened sponge and top with flaked chocolate. Dust with sifted cocoa. Chill for several hours or overnight before serving.

CHOCOLATE MARQUISE

The Marquise is a grand figure in society and provides inspiration for this extravagant cake bedecked with a chocolate frill.

SERVES 4

soft butter for greasing

2 eggs, at room temperature

50 g / 2 oz / ¼ cup caster (superfine) sugar

45 ml / 3 tbsp plain (all-purpose) flour

15 ml / 1 tbsp cornflour (cornstarch)

30 ml / 2 tbsp cocoa

For the filling

150 g / 5 oz plain (semi-sweet) chocolate

2 eggs, separated

30 ml / 2 tbsp dark rum or Grand Marnier

30 ml / 2 tbsp caster (superfine) sugar

200 ml / 7 floz / ¾ cup double (heavy) cream, loosely whipped

To decorate

225 g / 8 oz plain (semi-sweet) chocolate

50 g / 2 oz white covering chocolate

Preheat the oven to 190°C / 375°F / Gas 5. Grease an 18 cm / 7 in loose-bottomed cake tin (pan). Line with greaseproof (wax) paper and dust the sides with flour. Whisk the eggs and sugar until thick. Fold in the flour, cornflour (cornstarch) and cocoa. Turn into the tin (pan). Bake for 25 minutes until springy to the touch.

Turn onto a wire rack. When cool, slice in half. Line the sides of the cake tin (pan) with a strip of greaseproof (wax) paper and put one layer of sponge on the base of the pan (the second layer is not needed).

To make the filling, melt the chocolate, then stir in the egg yolks and the alcohol. Whisk the egg whites until stiff, add the sugar and whisk to form peaks. Stir a spoonful of egg white into the chocolate, then fold the chocolate into the whites. Fold in the cream and put into the tin (pan). Chill.

For the decoration, temper the plain chocolate as described on page 77 and spread half onto a smooth work surface, keeping the rest molten. Remove the marquise from the tin. Before the chocolate has completely set, scrape it into strips and place on top of the cream. Melt the white chocolate. Lay out a strip of thin plastic or acetate 6 cm / 2 ½ in wide and pipe on a wavy line of melted white chocolate. Spread an even layer of melted plain chocolate on top. When almost set, lift the strip by each end and wrap around the marquise. When set, remove the plastic.

$\mathscr{H}$AZELNUT MERINGUE

Abandon your principles and sink into this hotbed of chocolate meringue, sighing with hazelnut cream and spun sugar.

SERVES 4-6

2 egg whites, at room temperature

115 g / 4 oz / ½ cup caster
(superfine) sugar

15 g / ½ oz hazelnuts, toasted

2 tsp cocoa

60 ml / 4 tbsp chocolate hazelnut
spread

15 ml / 1 tbsp boiling water

300 ml / ½ pint / 1¼ cups double
(heavy) cream, loosely whipped

For the spun sugar decoration

150 g / 5 oz / ⅔ cup caster
(superfine) sugar

gold leaf (optional)

small chocolate curls

Preheat the oven to 120°C / 250°F / Gas ½. Line two large baking sheets with clean brown paper, then cover with non-stick baking paper. Draw 4 x 13 cm / 5 in circles. Whisk the egg whites until stiff, then whisk in the sugar until stiff and glossy. Fold in the chopped hazelnuts and cocoa. Divide the mixture between the circles, and bake for 2-3 hours.

Mix the chocolate spread and water; cool. Fold into the cream. Allow the meringues to cool, then sandwich with the cream mixture.

To make the spun sugar, first spread newspaper on the floor. Put 30 ml / 2 tbsp of the sugar into a heavy pan. Heat and stir until the sugar melts. Add the rest gradually, stirring constantly until dissolved. Do not leave unattended. When the sugar has lightly caramelized, put the base of the pan in cold water. Using a fork, spin threads of sugar over a long rolling pin held out straight. Collect the sugar into a fleece and wrap around the meringue. Decorate with gold leaf (if using) and chocolate curls.

EXPLODING CHOCOLATE BOMBE SHELL

Layers of white and dark chocolate filling encompass a central charge of amaretti mascarpone cream. Frozen bombes take time to prepare, but can be made well in advance.

SERVES 6-8

For the pâte à bombe
3 egg yolks
75 g / 3 oz / ⅓ cup caster
  (superfine) sugar
15 ml / 1 tbsp water

For the sponge
3 eggs
75 g / 3 oz / ⅓ cup caster
  (superfine) sugar
30 ml / 2 tbsp cornflour (cornstarch)
45 ml / 3 tbsp ground almonds
60 ml / 4 tbsp cocoa

For the outer layer
15 ml / 1 tbsp caster (superfine) sugar
30 ml / 2 tbsp boiling water
150 g / 5 oz white chocolate, broken
  into pieces

15 g / ½ oz maraschino cherries,
  quartered
15 g / ½ oz unsalted pistachio nuts,
  skinned
300 ml / ½ pint / 1¼ cups whipping
  cream, loosely whipped

For the second layer
15 ml / 1 tbsp caster (superfine) sugar
45 ml / 3 tbsp boiling water
115 g / 4 oz plain (semi-sweet)
  chocolate, broken into pieces
15 g / ½ oz / 2 tbsp raisins
100 ml / 4 fl oz / ½ cup whipping
  cream, loosely whipped

For the centre filling
25 g / 1 oz amaretti biscuits, broken
125 g / 4 oz mascarpone cheese
30 ml / 2 tbsp Maraschino or Kirsch

To finish
*150 ml / ¼ pint / ⅔ cup whipping
cream, stiffly whipped*

To make the pâte à bombe, whisk the egg yolks in the bowl of an electric mixer until thick and foamy. Place the sugar and water in a small heavy saucepan and heat to dissolve, then boil to 116°C / 240°F on a sugar thermometer. Whisk the egg yolks again, slowly pour in the boiling sugar and continue whisking for 2-3 minutes until smooth. Measure 50 g / 2 oz and 25 g / 1 oz of the mixture into two separate bowls.

Preheat the oven to 200°C / 400°F / Gas 6. Line a 33 x 25 cm / 13 x 10 in Swiss roll (jelly roll) tray with greaseproof (wax) paper. For the sponge, whisk the eggs and sugar together until thick and foamy. Fold in the dry ingredients. Spread into the tray and bake for 10-12 minutes. Cool.

To make the outer layer, put a 1.1 liter / 2 pint bombe mould in the freezer to chill. Dissolve the sugar in the boiling water, add the chocolate and stir until melted. Add the

cherries and pistachios and leave to cool. Add the whipped cream and fold in gently with 50 g / 2 oz of the prepared pâte à bombe. Spread the mixture into the bombe mould with the back of a spoon to make an even layer. Freeze for 2 hours.

To make the second layer, dissolve the sugar in the boiling water, add the chocolate and stir until melted. Add the raisins and leave to cool. Then fold in the whipped cream and 25 g / 1 oz of the pâte à bombe. Spread the mixture over the outer layer in the mould and freeze for 2 hours.

To make the centre filling, combine the amaretti biscuits with the mascarpone and moisten with the alcohol. Spoon into the central cavity of the bombe mould. Cover the mould with a circle cut out of the chocolate sponge and freeze for 1 hour.

To decorate, dip the bombe mould in hot water for a few seconds and turn out. With a long knife, slice away the top surface of the remaining sponge and dice finely. Spread the bombe with whipped cream, cover with the diced sponge and serve.

DEVIL'S FOOD CAKE

*Devil's Food Cake - a very apt name for this sinfully rich
and delicious chocolate temptation.*

SERVES 4-6

For the cake
soft butter for greasing
75 ml / 3 floz / ⅓ cup water
15 ml / 1 tbsp clear honey
75 g / 3 oz plain (semi-sweet)
    chocolate, broken into pieces
150 g / 5 oz / ⅔ cup unsalted (sweet)
    butter, softened
175 g / 6 oz / ¾ cup caster
    (superfine) sugar
3 eggs, separated
115 g / 4 oz / 1 cup self-raising (self-
    rising) flour
90 ml / 6 tbsp cocoa

For the icing
150 ml / ¼ pint / ⅔ cup fresh single
    (light) cream
175 g / 6 oz plain (semi-sweet)
    chocolate, broken into pieces
15 ml / 1 tbsp caster (superfine) sugar
75 g / 3 oz / ⅓ cup unsalted (sweet)
    butter, softened

Preheat the oven to 180°C / 350°F /
Gas 4. Grease a 20 cm / 8in
angel cake tin (pan) with butter.
Bring the water and honey to the boil
to make a syrup. Remove from the
heat and stir in the chocolate.

Beat the butter with 150 g / 5 oz /
⅔ cup of the sugar. Add the egg yolks
and sift in the flour and cocoa. Stir in
the chocolate mixture.

Whisk the egg whites until stiff.
Add the remaining sugar and whisk
until firm. Fold the egg whites into
the chocolate mixture and turn into
the tin (pan). Bake for 40 minutes.
Leave to cool for 10-15 minutes
before turning out to cool completely.

To make the icing, bring the cream
almost to the boil, remove from heat,
add the chocolate, sugar and butter
and stir until melted. Pour the icing
over the cake to coat it evenly and
leave to set.

FUDGENUT CHOCOLATE PUDDING

Fast for a week - this pudding is not for the faint hearted! One spoonful will lead to another and another and ...

SERVES 4

For the pudding

soft butter for greasing

150 g / 5 oz plain (semi-sweet)
  chocolate, broken into pieces

45 ml / 3 tbsp dark rum

4 eggs, separated

115 g / 4 oz / ½ cup caster
  (superfine) sugar

75 g / 3 oz / ¾ cup ground almonds

75 g / 3 oz / 1½ cups fresh white
  breadcrumbs

50 g / 2 oz vanilla fudge, diced

For the sauce

150 ml / ¼ pint / ⅔ cup fresh single
  (light) cream

15 ml / 1 tbsp caster (superfine)
  sugar

175g / 6 oz plain (semi-sweet)
  chocolate

Grease a 900 ml / 1½ pint / 3¾ cup pudding basin with butter and set aside. Melt the chocolate in a large bowl set over a saucepan of gently simmering water. Stir in the rum and egg yolks. Whisk the egg whites in another large bowl until stiff, then gradually add the sugar, whisking until firm. Combine the ground almonds, breadcrumbs and fudge, then fold into the whisked egg whites. Stir a spoonful of this mixture into the melted chocolate, then fold in the remainder using a metal spoon.

Turn the mixture into the buttered basin, cover the surface with a circle of greaseproof (wax) paper, then cover the basin tightly with foil. Stand the basin in a deep saucepan partly filled with simmering water, cover

and steam for 1 hour 20 minutes, topping up the pan with more boiling water as necessary.

To make the sauce, rinse a saucepan with cold water, add the cream and sugar and bring almost to the boil. Remove from heat, add the chocolate and stir to melt. Turn out the pudding and serve with the hot chocolate sauce.

CHOCOLATE AND GINGER SUNDAE

Wanted: two people to share spacious ice cream sundae. Fitted with chocolate, ginger cake and cream throughout.

SERVES 2

75 g / 3 oz ginger bread

50 g / 2 oz stem (preserved) ginger in syrup

150 ml / ¼ pint / ⅔ cup whipping cream

15 ml / 1 tbsp caster (superfine) sugar

30 ml / 2 tbsp Grand Marnier (optional)

500 ml / 18 floz chocolate ice cream

1 glacé cherry

2 pieces of candy

75 ml / 3 floz / ⅓ cup whipped cream

2 milk chocolate flakes

Cut the ginger bread into slices, then moisten it with the ginger syrup. Loosely whip the cream in a clean bowl, sweeten with the sugar and flavour with Grand Marnier (if using).

Put alternate layers of ginger bread, chocolate ice cream and ginger-flavoured cream in a large sundae glass (or, if you prefer, use 2 individual sundae glasses).

Cut 2 pieces of stem ginger into heart shapes and cut the glacé cherry in half, using a zig-zag motion, to form 'flowers'. Thread onto fancy skewers or cocktail sticks (toothpicks) and top each with a piece of candy. Decorate the sundae with whipped cream, the chocolate flakes and the filled skewers.

$\mathscr{H}$OT CHOCOLATE SOUFFLÉ

Learning to make a soufflé is like riding a bicycle. Once you have managed the upright position, the future is paved with success.

SERVES 4

For the dish

soft butter for greasing

a little caster (superfine) sugar for dusting

For the soufflé

300 ml / ½ pint / 1¼ cups milk

6 eggs, separated

75 ml / 5 tbsp caster (superfine) sugar

60 ml / 4 tbsp plain (all-purpose) flour

30 ml / 2 tbsp cocoa

30 ml / 2 tbsp dark rum

50 g / 2 oz plain (semi-sweet) chocolate chips

icing (confectioner's) sugar for dusting

Choose a 900 ml / 1½ pint / 3¾ cup soufflé dish or 4 x 300 ml / ½ pint / 1¼ cups soufflé dishes. Preheat the oven to 190°c / 375°F / Gas 5. Smear a thin, even layer of soft butter on the inside of the dishes using 2 fingers. Dust with caster (superfine) sugar and set aside.

Measure 50 ml / 2 floz / ¼ cup of the milk into a bowl. Add the egg yolks, 30 ml / 2 tbsp of the sugar, the flour, cocoa and rum and combine smoothly. Bring the remainder of the milk to the boil, pour over the egg mixture and stir evenly. Return the mixture to the saucepan and stir over a moderate heat to thicken. Cover to keep hot.

In a separate bowl, whisk the egg whites until firm. Gradually add the remaining 45 ml / 3 tbsp sugar, whisking until stiff. Stir a spoonful of whisked egg whites into the hot cocoa mixture and whisk briefly to ensure a smooth texture. Fold the remaining cocoa mixture and the chocolate chips into the egg whites using a large metal spoon.

Turn the mixture into the prepared soufflé dish or dishes. Bake the large soufflé for 20 minutes or the smaller soufflés for 8 minutes. (Make sure your guests are assembled as soon as the soufflé comes out of the oven.) Dust the surface of the soufflé or soufflés with sifted icing (confectioner's) sugar and serve immediately.

CHOCOLATE FACTS ...AND FICTION

Many chocolate myths contain more than a grain of truth.

Some people claim that partaking of chocolate leads to an intensity of feeling akin to being in love. Scientists are now finding that there may be some truth in this. Pure chocolate contains phenylethylamine, a chemical produced by the body which contributes to that giddy 'high' associated with being in love. It is probably no coincidence that chocolates have been the traditional gift to a sweetheart for many years.

One of the characteristics that makes chocolate so delectable is surely its glorious melt-in-the-mouth quality. Because cocoa butter is solid at room temperature but has a melting point just below body temperature, chocolate readily melts when you place a piece in your mouth, giving you the full flavour. Why we enjoy this sensation is not clear – butter, cream and mayonnaise also have a similar effect, although the sensation surely finds its full expression with chocolate.

Chocolate is recognized to be one of the most perfect of foods. It is rich in carbohydrates, vegetable oils, protein, calcium, B vitamins and several minerals including iron. Chocolate contains theobromine, a mild stimulant similar to caffeine (which is also present in chocolate). For some unlucky people, chocolate can trigger headaches and migraine attacks. This may be due to tyramine, which can cause blood vessels in the head to constrict.

Many have considered chocolate to be a powerful aphrodisiac. It was the custom of the Aztec emperor, Montezuma II, to drink a golden bowl of the frothing liquid to increase his strength and wisdom before entering his harem.

Today, the most sought after chocolate comes from Belgium and France. Particularly the Belgians have dedicated themselves to perfecting the art of chocolate creation, and Liège is home to world-famous Godiva chocolates. England, not previously renowned for the manufacture of fine chocolates, is beginning to establish a reputation in the confectionery field. The Quakers regarded chocolate as a possible alternative to alcohol, and many of the first chocolate companies, such as Fry's and Cadbury's in England, were founded by wealthy Quaker families in the hope of curbing drunkenness.

STORING CHOCOLATE

Chocolate quickly absorbs odours and should never be exposed to damp. Ideally it should be stored, well-wrapped, in an airtight container in a cool place. Chocolate bars now have an expiration date on the wrapper, so do check before eating or using it – it's not worth spoiling a recipe if the chocolate is past its best.

Stollwerck's Adler-Cacao.

CHOCOLATE CHIP COOKIES

Homemade chocolate chip cookies are an American institution. This all-in-one recipe makes a batch of cookies in next to no time.

MAKES 12

soft butter for greasing

½ tsp salt

115 g / 4 oz / ¾ cup soft light brown
   sugar

75 g / 3 oz / ⅓ cup unsalted (sweet)
   butter, softened

50 g / 2 oz / 3 tbsp smooth peanut
   butter

1 egg

½ tsp vanilla essence (extract)

150 g / 5 oz / 1¼ cups self-raising
   (self-rising) flour

75 g / 3 oz plain chocolate chips

P reheat the oven to 190°C /
   375°F / Gas 5. Grease 2 baking
sheets with soft butter and set aside.

   In a mixing bowl beat the sugar,
butters, egg and vanilla essence
together. Sift the flour and salt into
the bowl and beat with a wooden
spoon until smooth. Stir in the
chocolate chips.

   Drop tablespoonfuls of the
mixture onto the baking sheets,
spacing them 5 cm / 2 in apart.
Flatten each cookie with a palette
knife (spatula). Bake 1 tray at a time
for 10-12 minutes.

   Cool briefly, then lift with a
palette knife (spatula) onto a wire
rack and leave to cool. The cookies
will keep in an airtight container for
up to 10 days.

TWO-TONE CHOCOLATE MUFFINS

Bake these richly flavoured muffins in small tins - this way people can eat as many as they like without fear of overindulgence.

MAKES 24

75 g / 3 oz white chocolate, broken
  into pieces
75 g / 3 oz plain (semi-sweet)
  chocolate, broken into pieces
60 ml / 4 tbsp rum, whisky or Grand
  Marnier
50 g / 2 oz / ¼ cup unsalted (sweet)
  butter, softened
50 g / 2 oz / ¼ cup caster (superfine)
  sugar
50 g / 2 oz white marzipan, warmed
3 eggs, at room temperature, beaten
115 g / 4 oz / 1 cup self-raising
  (self-rising) flour
a pinch of salt
finely grated zest (rind) of ½ orange

Preheat the oven to 180°C / 350°F / Gas 4. You will need a small non-stick muffin tray with 24 indentations. Line with paper muffin cases if the tray is not of the non-stick variety.

Melt the white and dark chocolate in separate bowls set over 2 saucepans of gently simmering water. Add 30 ml / 2 tbsp alcohol to each bowl and stir. In a third bowl, blend the butter, sugar and marzipan together. Beat in the eggs a little at a time, then add the sifted flour, salt and the orange zest (rind). Stir just to combine.

Divide the mixture in half and stir the melted white chocolate into one portion and the dark chocolate into the remaining portion. Fill the muffin cases three-quarters full with spoonfuls of alternate coloured batter. Bake for 20-25 minutes until well risen and springy to the touch.

CHOCOLATE PECAN BROWNIES

Lingeringly chewy, moist and delicious.
One Chocolate Pecan Brownie is rarely enough ...

MAKES 9 SQUARES

115 g / 4 oz plain (semi-sweet)
chocolate, broken into pieces
115 g / 4 oz / ½ cup unsalted (sweet)
butter, cut into pieces
175 g / 6 oz / 1 cup soft light brown
sugar
2 eggs, beaten
50 g / 2 oz / ½ cup plain (all-
purpose) flour
1½ tsp baking powder
a pinch of salt
50 g / 2 oz / ½ cup chopped pecan
nuts

Preheat the oven to 180°C / 350°F / Gas 4. Lightly oil a 23 cm / 9 in square cake tin (pan) and line the base with greaseproof (wax) paper.

Melt the chocolate in a mixing bowl set over a saucepan of gently simmering water. Remove from the heat, add the butter and sugar and stir with a wooden spoon to soften, then stir in the eggs. Add the sifted flour, baking powder and salt, then add the nuts and stir well. Turn into the lined cake tin (pan) and bake for 30 minutes.

Cool, then cut into squares or rectangles. The brownies will keep in an airtight container for up to 10 days.

CHOCOLATE PROFIT-ÉCLAIRS

*A tempting tower of dainty cream-filled éclairs
with a generous topping of rich chocolate sauce.*

SERVES 4

For the choux pastry

225 ml / 8 fl oz / 1 cup water

50 g / 2 oz / ¼ cup butter

*115 g / 4 oz / 1 cup plain (all-
purpose) flour*

3 eggs, beaten

For the chocolate sauce

*150 ml / ¼ pint / ⅔ cup single (light)
cream*

15 ml / 1 tbsp caster (superfine) sugar

*175 g / 6 oz plain (semi-sweet)
chocolate*

For the filling

*300 ml / ½ pint / 1¼ cups whipping
cream*

30 ml / 2 tbsp vanilla sugar

P reheat the oven to 200°C /
400°F / Gas 6. Lightly grease
2 baking sheets. To make the pastry,
boil the water and butter in a heavy
saucepan. Add the flour and stir until
a smooth dough is formed. Transfer
to a bowl and cool briefly. Gradually
add the eggs and beat until smooth.

Using a piping (icing) bag fitted
with a 1 cm / ½ in plain nozzle, pipe
about 30 éclair shapes 5 cm / 2 in
long and 2.5 cm / 1 in apart onto the
baking sheets. Bake 1 sheet at a time
for 30-35 minutes until crisp.

To make the sauce, bring the cream
and sugar almost to the boil. Remove
from the heat, add the chocolate and
stir until melted.

To make the filling, whip the cream
with the sugar. Cut open the éclairs
and, using a 1 cm / ½ in nozzle, pipe
cream into each. To serve, dip the top
of each éclair in the chocolate sauce
and arrange in a serving dish.

CHOCOLATE DOG

*Inexperienced cook needed to create cake
from biscuits and melted chocolate. Stamina required.*

MAKES 1 LOAF

*400 g / 14 oz good quality plain (semi-
sweet) chocolate, broken into pieces*
*250 g / 9 oz digestive biscuits (graham
crackers), broken into pieces*

For the decoration
chocolate finger biscuits
tiny chocolate dragées
a little melted chocolate for fixing

L ine a small loaf tin (pan)
with cling film (plastic wrap).
Melt the chocolate in a bowl set

over a saucepan of gently simmering
water.

Add the broken biscuits (crackers)
to the melted chocolate, stir to
combine and turn into the prepared
tin (pan). Chill for about 30 minutes
or until set.

Turn out the chocolate, remove the
film (wrap) and cut into slices, cutting
some slices in half to form the 'heads'
if you wish. Press a piece of chocolate
finger biscuit into position to form
the 'eyes' and finish with tiny
chocolate dragées, fixed in place with
melted chocolate.

To assemble the 'dogs', fix the
'heads' into position on the 'body'
slices using a little melted chocolate.
Cut chocolate finger biscuits in half
and, using a little melted chocolate,
attach one to each 'dog' to form the
'tail'. Leave to set before serving.

WHISKY TRUFFLES

Almost any spirit or liquor can be put into homemade chocolates.
Whisky is a favourite and is used to create a delicious confection.

MAKES 36 TRUFFLES

For the filling

225 g / 8 oz good quality plain (semi-
    sweet) chocolate, broken into
    pieces
45 ml / 3 tbsp double (heavy) cream
45 ml / 3 tbsp whisky

For the coating

225 g / 8 oz good quality plain (semi-
    sweet) chocolate, broken into pieces

To make the filling, melt the chocolate in a bowl set over a saucepan of simmering water. Stir in the cream and whisky until evenly blended. Allow to cool to room temperature and set. (Chill slightly to help in warm weather, but ensure that the mixture remains smooth.)

Line a tray with greaseproof (wax) paper. Spoon the mixture into thumb-sized pieces and chill to firm. When firm, roll into neat balls and return to the fridge.

Melt the coating chocolate as before. Take only a few filling balls at a time to prevent the others softening. Using a fork, dip one ball at a time into the melted chocolate to coat and leave to set on a sheet of greaseproof (wax) paper. Place in paper cases and keep in a cool, dry place.

CHAMPAGNE TRUFFLES

True Champagne truffles are flavoured with Cognac, rather than with the bubbly Champagne from northern France. The finest Cognac matures in the region of La Grande Champagne in the southwest.

MAKES 36 TRUFFLES

For the filling

250 g / 9 oz good quality plain (semi-sweet) chocolate, broken into pieces

45 ml / 3 tbsp double (heavy) cream

45 ml / 3 tbsp finest Cognac

For the coating

225 g / 8 oz good quality plain (semi-sweet) chocolate, broken into pieces

45 ml / 3 tbsp icing (confectioner's) sugar

To make the filling, melt the chocolate in a bowl set over a saucepan of simmering water. Stir in the cream and Cognac until evenly blended. Leave to cool to room temperature and set. (Chill slightly to help in warm weather, but ensure that the mixture remains smooth.)

Line a tray with greaseproof (wax) paper. Place the filling in a piping (icing) bag fitted with a 1 cm / ½ in star nozzle, then pipe the mixture into long lengths on the paper. Chill to firm.

To prepare the coating, slowly melt the chocolate in a bowl set over a saucepan of gently simmering water, making sure that the chocolate is no hotter than a finger can bear.

Cut the filling into 4 cm / 1½ in lengths and return all but a few of the truffle shapes back to the fridge to prevent them from softening. Spread the icing (confectioner's) sugar onto a large plate. Using a fork, dip one truffle at a time into the melted chocolate, then roll them in icing (confectioner's) sugar. Store in a cool, dry place.

*D*IPPED DELICACIES

Dainty morsels coated in rich chocolate satisfy even the incurable chocoholic's cravings for something sweet.

MAKES ABOUT 30

For the coating

350 g / 12 oz good quality plain (semi-sweet) chocolate, broken into pieces

For the fillings

50 g / 2 oz whole almonds

50 g / 2 oz whole brazil nuts

50 g / 2 oz dates, pitted

50 g / 2 oz marzipan

To prepare the coating, temper the chocolate following the method described on page 77. Once the chocolate has been returned to the bowl set over simmering water, select a nut and dip it into the chocolate using a fork or your fingers. Once the nut is completely coated, shake off any excess chocolate and place on greaseproof (wax) paper to set. Repeat the dipping process until all the nuts are covered in chocolate.

Next, open the dates and stuff each one with a little roll shape of marzipan. Dip the stuffed dates into the chocolate one by one, repeating the process until all have been coated. Leave to set on greaseproof (wax) paper.

*T*WO CHOCOLATE FUDGES

Both white and dark chocolate are used to make these exotic fudges which include pistachios, cherries and rum-soaked raisins.

MAKES 675 G / 1½ LB OF EACH FUDGE

soft butter, for greasing

For the dark fudge

25 g / 1 oz / ¼ cup raisins

30 ml / 2 tbsp dark rum

450 g / 1 lb / 2 cups granulated sugar

75 ml / 3 fl oz / ⅓ cup milk

50 g / 2 oz / ¼ cup unsalted (sweet) butter

175 g / 6 oz plain (semi-sweet) chocolate

For the white fudge

450 g / 1 lb / 2 cups granulated sugar

75 ml / 3 fl oz / ⅓ cup milk

50 g / 2 oz / ¼ cup unsalted (sweet) butter

175 g / 6 oz white chocolate, broken into pieces

25 g / 1 oz unsalted skinned pistachios

15 g / ½ oz / 1 tbsp glacé cherries

Butter 2 shallow 20 cm / 8 in square tins (pans). Soak the raisins in the rum for 1 hour.

To make the dark fudge, heat the sugar and milk and stir over a moderate heat until the sugar is dissolved. Add the butter and plain (semi-sweet) chocolate, then stir until the temperature reaches 110°C / 230°F on a sugar thermometer. Add the raisins and rum. Turn into one of the tins (pans), level the surface and leave to set.

To make the white fudge, heat the sugar and milk and stir over a moderate heat until the sugar is dissolved. Add the butter and white chocolate, then stir until the temperature reaches 110°C / 230°F on a sugar thermometer. Add the pistachios and cherries. Turn into the remaining tin (pan), and leave to set as before. To serve, cut each fudge into squares.

HOT CHOCOLATE TODDY

*Consenting adults need little help plumbing the depths
of this alcoholic chocolate dream.*

SERVES 2

*115 g / 4 oz good quality plain (semi-
sweet) chocolate, broken into
pieces*

1 egg yolk

30 ml / 2 tbsp dark rum

½ tsp mustard powder (optional)

200 ml / 7 floz / ¾ cup milk

*120 ml / 4 floz / ½ cup single (light)
cream*

For the topping

whipped cream

drinking chocolate powder

P lace the chocolate, egg yolk,
rum and mustard (if desired)
in a blender and whip (the small
amount of mustard powder will
enhance the chocolate without
spoiling the taste).

Rinse a small pan with cold water,
then add the milk and cream and
bring to a simmer. Blend the milk
with the chocolate mixture until
frothy. Pour into two heatproof
glasses or mugs, top with whipped
cream and dust with drinking
chocolate powder.

DECORATING WITH CHOCOLATE

Chocolate can be used in a variety of interesting and attractive ways to decorate cakes, biscuits, desserts and confectionery.

FLAKED CHOCOLATE OR CHOCOLATE CURLS

Chocolate flakes or curls look elegant, and are quick and easy to prepare. Use a thick bar of chocolate at room temperature – if it is too cold and hard the chocolate will break and if it is too warm and soft the curls will not hold their shape. Use a sharp potato peeler and peel/shave the chocolate bar into pretty flakes: for large flakes, shave the chocolate from the flat, unridged side (or the back of the bar) and for small flakes, turn the

bar on its side and shave along the narrow edge.

When decorating, lift the curls with the point of a knife so that they do not melt on contact with your fingers.

CHOCOLATE SHAVINGS

These long, luscious curls of chocolate always look spectacular. Melt covering chocolate or use tempered chocolate (see the method on the opposite page). Turn the warm chocolate onto a cold, flat surface (such as a marble slab or formica top) and spread out evenly to a thickness of less than 5 mm / ¼ in. Let the chocolate cool until it is on the verge of setting (but still pliable).

Using a long, sharp knife held at an angle of about 45°, push the blade away from you across the chocolate to shave off long curls. For smaller curls, use a short-bladed knife, and proceed in the same way.

Refrigerating the curls will help prevent their being damaged. Transfer them to the fridge on a sheet of greaseproof (wax) paper.

Chocolate Leaves

Chocolate leaves are an impressive decoration and are not at all difficult to make. Wash and dry the leaves to be used – rose leaves are ideal because of their classic shape and prominent veining. Dip the underside of each leaf into melted chocolate to give an even coating (or you can brush the leaves with melted chocolate, if you prefer). Leave to set hard on greaseproof (wax) paper, then carefully peel off the leaves

and discard. Use the chocolate leaves as desired.

To Temper Chocolate

To enable good quality chocolate to set so that it will snap cleanly between the teeth, it must be prepared in a special way known as tempering. (For quicker but less pleasing results use plain chocolate drops or cake-covering chocolate which set without special handling.)

To temper chocolate, melt it in a bowl set over a pan of simmering water, ensuring that the chocolate is no hotter than a finger will bear. Turn out onto a clean, dry, smooth surface or marble slab. Spread with a palette knife (spatula) until firm but not completely set. Return to the bowl and heat very gently for 5-10 seconds, stirring well until it reaches an even consistency. If the temperature rises above 30°C / 88°F, the chocolate will not set firmly later.